Queen of the Mountain

TAK Erzinger

Text copyright © TAK Erzinger 2024
Illustrations copyright © TAK Erzinger 2024
All rights reserved.

ISBN Paperback: 978-1-83584-011-5
ISBN Hardback: 978-1-83584-012-8
ISBN eBook: 978-1-83584-010-2

TAK Erzinger has asserted her right under the Copyright, Designs and Patent Act 1988 to be identified as the author of this work.

This is a work of fiction. Names, characters, businesses, places, events and incidents are either the products of the author's imagination or used in a fictitious manner. Any resemblance to actual persons, living or dead, or actual events is purely coincidental.

First published 2024
by Rowanvale Books Ltd
The Gate
Keppoch Street
Roath
Cardiff
CF24 3JW
www.rowanvalebooks.com
Library Cataloguing in Publication Data.
A catalogue record for this book is available from the British Library.

All rights reserved. No part of this book may be reprinted or reproduced or utilised in any form or by electronic, mechanical or any other means, now known or hereafter invented, including photocopying or recording, or in any information storage or retrieval system, without the permission in writing from the Publishers.

For Grandmommy and Abuela.

There's a place where the mountains are so high, they look like they kiss the sky.

Vicky's world **runs** through these mountains, lakes and streams. With her father, she lives in harmony with **nature**.

One day, a strange group arrives in Vicky's small village.

At the centre of this group is a short and round lady. Everyone is fussing about her. **She seems important. She looks sad.**

Curious, Vicky asks the lady, "Who are you?"

She replies, "I'm the Countess of Kent."

Standing proudly, Vicky tells her,
"I'm Victoria, but you can call me Vicky."

Suddenly, the sad lady smiles. Her eyes twinkle like stars.

"She's very **fancy**," comments Vicky's father.

"And **sad**," Vicky replies.

They decide to try and **cheer up** the little stranger.

Vicky makes a bouquet of **flowers** from their farmer's garden.

The centrepiece is made up of roses. She leaves them at the reception of the inn.

The countess is very surprised to find a bouquet of beautiful Alpen flowers, especially including so many roses.

Early in the mornings, the countess goes out on her **horse**, and a few people follow her, carrying what she needs. Vicky follows at a distance. She watches everything. She notices that the countess sits for **hours** in the same places that Vicky loves.

Sometimes, she stares out at the sights, sometimes painting, sometimes sleeping. One day, while the countess is taking a nap on the hillside, Vicky **creeps** over to see what she has painted.

It is the lovely landscape, seen through a window, featuring the bouquet of flowers Vicky gave her.

The painting is **beautiful**, Vicky thinks.

Just as she reaches out to touch it, the countess **wakes up!** The countess **scares** Vicky, and she tries to **run** away, but then the countess says, "Come here, child," in a **soft**, nice voice.

After a moment, she asks Vicky, "Do you like my painting?"

Vicky answers shyly, "Yes, **very much**."

The countess **reaches** out her hands and says, "Thank you for the **flowers**."

Vicky smiles widely and then asks, "Why are you **sad?**"

The countess answers, "Because someone I love **very much** died. His name was Albert."

"Oh," answers Vicky. "Someone I love died too, but it was my mother. She **loved** roses. The ones I gave you were from her garden."

The countess touches her **heart** and **smiles** back warmly at Vicky.

The countess gives Vicky her painting. Vicky can't wait to get **home** and **show** her father.

She **misses** her mother very much. It was nice to talk to the countess about her.

That evening, under the **stars**, the countess takes out a locket with dried rose petals inside from her pocket. She puts it next to a photo of Albert and whispers, "I'm **finally here**, and something has happened that makes me feel happy again. **Thank you**, Albert."

The rest of the week, Vicky spends the days with the countess. It is **warm** and **sunny**. The countess shares her food with Vicky, and they watch and enjoy the landscape. Sometimes, they **giggle**.

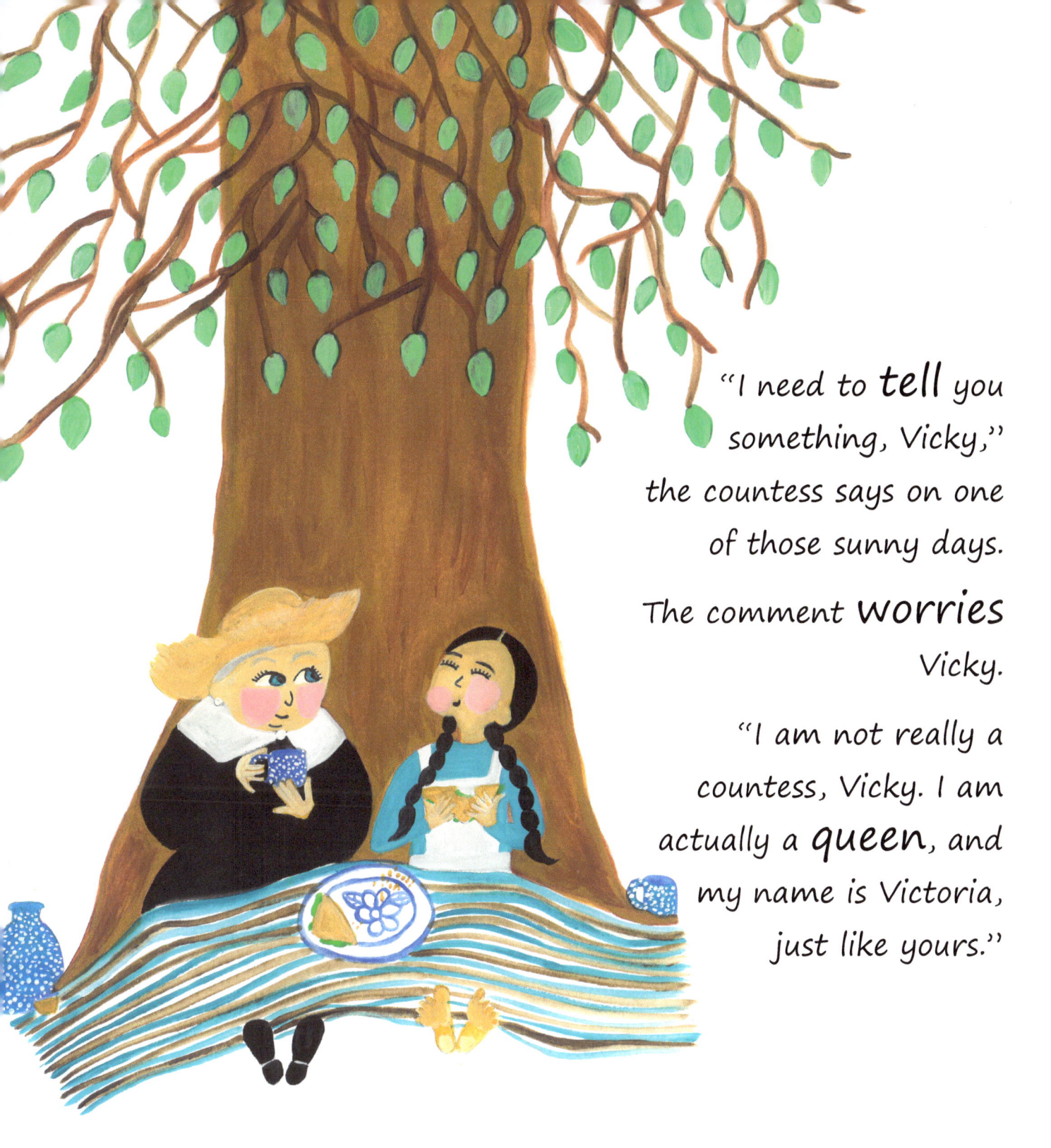

"I need to **tell** you something, Vicky," the countess says on one of those sunny days.

The comment **worries** Vicky.

"I am not really a countess, Vicky. I am actually a **queen**, and my name is Victoria, just like yours."

"A queen? Named Victoria?" Vicky giggles. She then says, "And I am Queen of the Mountain!" and laughs loudly.

The countess laughs, too. "I believe you are! But it is true, my name is Queen Victoria. I am the Queen of England."

Suddenly, Vicky becomes very sad. "But I am just a poor mountain girl, and you're a queen! I don't think we can be friends anymore. Besides, you are leaving soon." She turns around and runs away.

Vicky arrives home in **tears** and tells her father what happened.

"It's **okay**, Vicky," says her father. "Sometimes, people who are very different from each other can be friends. You make the little queen **very happy**, and she makes you **happy**, too."

That evening, Vicky dreams about Queen Victoria wearing a **large crown.** She is surrounded by roses and smiling with her arms open wide. There are **angels** beside her.

The next morning, there is a **knock** at the door. One of Queen Victoria's assistants has come with a delivery for Vicky. He announces, **"The Queen** requests to spend her last day here, with **Vicky."**

He has brought a **letter** beautifully written by the Queen, which smells like **roses**. It says, "I'm sorry I did not tell you the truth in the beginning. I cannot trust many people, but with you **I trust my heart**."

Vicky's father heats a bath for Vicky, shines up her shoes and presents her with a **beautiful** dress he had been saving for her birthday.

"Your mother would be **proud**," he says.

Vicky answers, "I'd like her even if she **wasn't** a queen."

"I know you would, Vicky, I know you would."

That afternoon, Queen Victoria and Vicky visit Mount Pilatus. For both, it feels like being in a **painting** or a **dream**.

When they return to the village, it is time for Queen Victoria to say **goodbye**, and Vicky feels **sad**.

"Vicky, I have a **present** for you," Queen Victoria says and hands her a small locket with rose petals inside. "Something for you to remember our **time together**."

Vicky replies shyly, "Thank you, but I don't have **anything** to give you."

Queen Victoria smiles brightly. "Oh, but you have already given me my present. You gave me the gift of **happiness**. And I thank you dearly, my Queen of the Mountain."

At that, Vicky hugs Queen Victoria, and they both whisper,

"Thank you."

Afterword

Queen Victoria was the Queen of England from 1837 to 1901. Her reign was called the Victorian Era. Queen Victoria married Prince Albert of Saxe-Coburg and Gotha in 1840. The two of them had nine children. Sadly, Prince Albert died in 1861. In the summer of 1868, Queen Victoria visited central Switzerland. She was still mourning the deep loss of her husband, Prince Albert. She decided to undertake this journey because the prince had once given her some dried roses he had collected in Switzerland, a place he was most fond of. Perhaps she felt that visiting a place he loved could offer her some much-needed comfort and quiet, to help her through the grieving process. During her five-week stay, she walked, rode horses and painted the natural landscapes of central Switzerland.

Queen of the Mountain is a fictionalised account of her time in Switzerland.

Author Profile

Photographer: Lisa Bertschinger

TAK Erzinger is an American/Swiss poet and artist with a Colombian background.

Her poetry has been featured in journals from Indiana University, Cornell University, McMaster University, the University of Baltimore and more. Erzinger's poetry collection At the Foot of the Mountain (Floricanto Press, 2021) won the University of Indianapolis Etchings Press Whirling Prize 2021 for best nature poetry book and was a finalist at The International Book Awards 2022. Her poetry collection Tourist (Sea Crow Press, 2023) was recently shortlisted as a finalist at the Eyelands Book Awards 2023. Erzinger was a writer-in-residence at the Art Centre Padula Residency Programme, summer 2023.

She lives in the foothills of the Swiss Alps with her husband and two cats.

***

If you have enjoyed this book, please take a few minutes to write a review of it online.

Thank you kindly.

Publisher Information

Rowanvale Books provides publishing services to independent authors, writers and poets all over the globe. We deliver a personal, honest and efficient service that allows authors to see their work published, while remaining in control of the process and retaining their creativity. By making publishing services available to authors in a cost-effective and ethical way, we at Rowanvale Books hope to ensure that the local, national and international community benefits from a steady stream of good quality literature.

For more information about us, our authors or our publications, please get in touch.
www.rowanvalebooks.com
info@rowanvalebooks.com